POWER
BOOK OF
LEADERSHIP

BYRD BAGGETT

RUTLEDGE HILL PRESS®

Nashville, Tennessee

Published in Nashville, Tennessee, by Rutledge Hill Press, Inc., 211 Seventh Avenue North, Nashville, Tennessee 37219.

Distributed in Canada by H. B. Fenn & Company, Ltd., 34 Nixon Road, Bolton, Ontario L7E 1W2.

Distributed in Australia by The Five Mile Press Pty., Ltd., 22 Summit Road, Noble Park, Victoria 3174.

Distributed in New Zealand by Tandem Press, 2 Rugby Road, Birkenhead, Auckland 10.

Distributed in the United Kingdom by Verulam Publishing, Ltd., 152a Park Street Lane, Park Street, St. Albans, Hertfordshire AL2 2AU.

Design by Gore Studios
Typography by Compass Communications, Inc., Nashville, Tennessee

ISBN: 1-55853-461-X
Printed in the Republic of China

2 3 4 5 6 7 8 9 – 02 01 00 99

INTRODUCTION

As I crisscross the country speaking to thousands of individuals, I am continually amazed by the reports I get confirming the vacuum of leadership in America. Few of those in charge seem to possess the tools needed to be powerful leaders–direction, motivation, action, and accountability.

The success of an organization has less to do with its product or service, than with how the organization develops and builds the soul of the firm–the employee. Organizations that understand and appreciate the value of servant leadership, in which those in charge submit themselves to the task-oriented needs of subordinates, will continue to prosper at the expense of establishments trapped by traditional management methods. This recognition of the vital role of servant leadership was the basis for my book *Taking Charge* and also serves as the essence of this power book, which is comprised of entries from *Taking Charge* as well as new common-sense tenets reflecting changing times and the need for desperate measures.

Corporate downsizing, creative stagnation, and unproductive like-mindedness provide an unprecedented opportunity for new leaders to step to the forefront. My hope is that this collection of insights will encourage you on your way to leadership success.

First and foremost, a good
leader serves others.

Your ability to serve
others starts with
mastering yourself.

Make finding a solution
a higher priority than
placing blame.

True leadership involves
not only the exercise of
authority, but also
full acceptance of
responsibility.

GOALS ARE DREAMS WITH DEADLINES.

Leaders solve today's problems while looking to tomorrow's opportunities.

Leaders see more in others than others see in themselves.

Praise in public.
Criticize in private.

LEAD means Learn,
Educate, Appreciate,
Develop.

Failure to take a risk is much worse than taking a risk that leads to failure.

Surround yourself with talent better than your own and carefully nurture it.

Most solutions are simple.

Leaders perform for
results, not recognition.

A leader's worst decision
is the one that is
never made.

Leaders learn from the past, focus on the present, and prepare for the future.

True leaders put the common good ahead of personal gain.

An in-person visit beats a
written memo every time.

A leader's state of mind
affects every person in
the organization.

Effective leaders are
blessed with a not-so-
common trait—
common sense.

Make important decisions
only when you are alert
and relaxed.

PROVIDE THE SKY IN WHICH OTHERS CAN SOAR.

Be teachable; you don't
know everything.

Coercion kills the
corporate spirit.

Listen to feedback
carefully.

A willingness to encourage change keeps you moving forward.

A leader is continually developing character and competence.

Lead people,
not organizations.

Trust your judgment and
be willing to act on it.

Be willing to sacrifice.

"I care about you." Say it, mean it, and live it.

Share your joy with others.

Take initiative and encourage others to do the same.

Expect people to perform only as well as the example you set.

A leader has a sense of
humility.

A leader has a sense of
history.

A leader has a sense of
humor.

True sincerity is a rare but valuable leadership trait.

Kindness
is not weakness.

Leaders inspire others to
motivate themselves.

Continue to work on your
communication skills–
both written and verbal.

Leaders look for great
ideas, not just consensus.

Lead a balanced life and
encourage the same in
those you lead.

Leaders can take charge
without being control
freaks.

Be accessible and
accountable.

Trust your gut feeling;
it's usually right.

"A soft answer turns away wrath" (Proverbs 15:1).

People-focused organizations create the best bottom-line results.

Ask your associates, "What would you do?" Expect powerful results.

Great reading on servant leadership: *The Soul of the Firm* by C. William Pollard (HarperBusiness).

Leadership is not taught within the walls of academia.

Good leadership is much deeper than personal appearance or rhetoric.

Always try to empower
others to do their best.

Winners are willing to
accept the risk others
are not.

Share your knowledge
with associates.

SET PRIORITIES
AND LIVE BY THEM.

Follow the channels of authority. And remember that it works both ways.

Before you critique another's behavior, list five positive things about that person.

Look for ways to make other people's jobs more challenging and fulfilling.

The number one request of employees: to be appreciated for a job well done.

ANTICIPATE CHAOS AND BE PREPARED TO WORK THROUGH IT.

Good leaders know how
to help others achieve
their full potential.

Decisions should be based
on the core values of an
organization.

Leaders have an innate
ability to bring out the best
in others.

Leaders realize that a
house divided will fall.

Organizations that encourage everyone's participation have an inside track to success.

Employees want to be heard and understood.

Focus on team victories,
not individual triumphs.

Learn from failure;
don't be crippled by it.

Your rules apply to
you, too.

Have a genuine concern
for those you lead.

Exert your will through
persuasion, not
intimidation.

Be firm but fair.

Greet everyone with
a smile and salutation
each morning.

You are in partnership
with the associates
you serve.

REAL LEADERS ARE MENTORS.

Listen with your heart as
well as your head.

A leader puts empathy
ahead of authority.

When trust is broken, all communication ceases.

Use your drive time to and from work to listen to motivational tapes.

A good decision today
beats the "perfect"
decision next week.

The path of least
resistance is not always
the best choice.

LEADERS INSPIRE; MANAGERS CONTROL.

Be real. Others know when you're just going through the motions of good leadership.

Change three bad habits a year–you will get phenomenal results!

Be willing to laugh at
yourself.

Seek wise counsel.

Leaders focus on guiding,
not ruling.

The acid test of an effective leader: Do you sleep well at night?

Time and energy spent worrying are wasted.

Simple philosophy:
If you serve others,
they will serve you!

Continue to find new
ways to support those
around you.

Do NOT LOWER
YOUR STANDARDS
TO ACCOMMODATE
OTHERS.

Know when to get out of
the way!

Manage procedures,
lead people.

Be courteous.

We are what we watch,
listen to, and read.

If necessary, agree
to disagree.

A true leader trains
others to lead.

Avoid the temptation to blame outside circumstances for your problems.

Keep a journal and write in it daily.

True loyalty is only that
which is volunteered.

Failure sends a leader in a
new direction toward his
or her next success.

LEADERSHIP
IS ABOUT
STEWARDSHIP,
NOT OWNERSHIP.

Don't feel you have to do it all yourself.

Watch out for the "squeaky wheel."

Envision goals as the targets and habits as the arrows.

Have zero tolerance for
negative attitudes.

A good plan has a clearly
defined objective clearly
communicated to
everyone.

CHALLENGES AND TESTS GO WITH THE TERRITORY.

Offer incentives that
encourage others to
take risks.

Learn from the past, but
don't be paralyzed by it.

Realize that we live in
the real world,
not an ideal one.

A group of people
committed to a shared
vision can accomplish
the impossible.

Reward performance and
recognize potential.

Leaders are willing to
swim upstream.

Those who outserve, out-
perform their competitors.

Be flexible.

Think of work as an
adventure and instill a
sense of exploration
in others.

ACCEPT BLAME AS WELL AS FAME.

Leaders understand the fragility and importance of others' self-esteem.

Instill confidence, not confusion, in those you lead.

A LEADER MUST EARN RESPECT, NOT DEMAND IT.

Remember that "silent" and "listen" contain the same letters.

Emulate the leadership habits of Vince Lombardi: discipline, hard work, and commitment.

Walk a mile in another person's shoes before passing judgment.

A leader tackles problems by helping associates choose the solution.

Put out a suggestion box, read the contents once a week, and act on them.

A shared philosophy and shared experiences sharpen your team's cohesion.

Always keep in mind that what others tell you is only the tip of the iceberg.

True rapport within an organization cannot be developed without a commitment to truth.

An open-door policy
should be exactly that.

Develop a spirit of
community, one individual
at a time.

Manage yourself;
lead others.

Choose what is right
instead of what is
politically correct.

Accept responsibility for
those you lead.

Use "we" instead of "me."

LEADERS ARE ORIGINALS, NOT DUPLICATES.

Be quick to throw a lifeline
to someone about to be
swept under.

The art of persuasion
begins with an open mind
and open ears, not an
open mouth.

Know the difference
between a rash decision
and a prompt one.

Tell those you lead what
they need to hear, not
what you think they
want to hear.

Roll up your sleeves and get your hands dirty.

Inside every person are seeds of greatness. Your task is to cultivate them.

Leaders are there when needed, not only when it is convenient for them.

Good leaders are like
baseball umpires: They go
practically unnoticed
when doing
their job right.

An apology is the sign of
a secure leader.

ALWAYS FOCUS ON THE BIG PICTURE.

Be serious about the
business, not about
yourself.

Accept people for who
and what they are,
regardless of how different
they are from you.

Be aware of an associate's obstacles to success, and work together to find the solutions.

∞

Leaders never put others on the firing line until they are ready.

Managers rely on manuals.
Leaders rely on instinct.

Allow ample time for
reflection and dreaming.

A leader always appears
calm and cool,
never confused.

Consult your conscience.

A good leader aspires to
be a role model rather than
a hero.

The abuse of power and
people will eventually
result in failure.

LEADERS PRACTICE WHAT THEY PREACH.

The trick in getting angry
is not losing your temper.

Mistakes are a necessary
part of the success process.

A leader balances logic
and emotion.

You must be yourself to be at peace.

You can lead a horse to water, but you can't manage him to drink.

Understand the importance of timing.

Encourage
PARTICIPATION.

Practice Stephen Covey's three character traits of greatness: integrity, maturity, and abundance mentality.

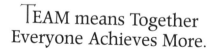

TEAM means Together Everyone Achieves More.

Employees who are given positive feedback work harder and accomplish more.

Leaders look at others as equals, not as subordinates.

Be consistently authentic and genuine. If you lose people's trust, it's almost impossible to regain it.

Don't let your ego get in the way.

Leaders respect those they
serve.

Be willing and prepared to
promote.

Keep in touch with the
work being done.

Share both the work and the wealth.

A reprimand should
build up, not tear down.

Encourage change and
new ideas. Don't be
intimidated by them.

Enthusiasm is a way of life,
not an emotion.

Small changes often
produce big results.

An organization's value
is measured as much by
the meaning it has for
its employees as it is
by net profits.

Build
Camaraderie.